The Language of Flowers
Coloring Book

John Green

DOVER PUBLICATIONS, INC.
Mineola, New York

Note

Prized for their beauty and grace, flowers have been a traditional gift for countless centuries. Colorful blooms have nestled themselves into the very fabric of many cultures, whether as thoughtful tokens, decorative ornaments, or medicinal aids. With an immeasurable number of types, sizes, varieties, and colors, it is no surprise that different flowers have come to represent certain emotions and sentiments over time, especially when given to others.

As with emotions, there are no fixed and definitive meanings for flowers, but the most common ones have been included here. Predictably, most of the traditional symbolism involves love—either its discovery or loss—and friendship. Though practices and customs may vary from region to generation, the pleasure and appreciation evoked by a gift of flowers is a universal constant.

The following thirty plates feature an assortment of lovely flowers, their traditional meanings, and their common colors.

Bibliographical Note

The Language of Flowers Coloring Book is a new work, first published
by Dover Publications, Inc., in 2003.

International Standard Book Number

ISBN-13: 978-0-486-43035-5
ISBN-10: 0-486-43035-9

Manufactured in the United States by RR Donnelley
43035916   2015
www.doverpublications.com

Dog Rose *(Rosa canina)*
Pleasure
White or pink petals with yellow centers

PLATE 1

Sweet Pea (*Lathyrus odoratus*)
Goodbye; thank you for a lovely time
Blue, pink, purple, red, or white

PLATE 2

Angelica *(Angelica venenosa)*
Inspiration; magic
White or greenish

PLATE 3

Orchid *(Laelia gouldiana)*
Beautiful lady; refinement
Red, purple, or magenta

PLATE 4

Lily *(Lilium candidum)*
Purity; sweetness; majesty
White petals with yellow-green centers

PLATE 5

Camellia *(Camellia japonica)*
You're adorable; without blemish; perfected loveliness
White

PLATE 6

Carnation *(Dianthus Emile Paré)*
I'll never forget you; fidelity
Pink

PLATE 7

Bluebell *(Hyacinthoides non-scripta)*
Humility; constancy
Blue

PLATE 8

Poppy *(Papaver orientale)*
Pleasure; fantastic; extravagance
Generally red, sometimes orange or pale pink

PLATE 9

Michaelmas Daisy *(Aster amellus 'sonia')*
Afterthought; farewell
Bright pink with yellow center

PLATE 10

Lilac *(Syringa vulgaris)*
Humility
Light purple, pink, or white

PLATE 11

Iris (*Iris germanica*)
Wisdom; valor; friendship; aflame; adversity
Many colors and combinations, such as pink, yellow, white, blue, and violet

PLATE 12

Magnolia *(Magnolia x soulangiana)*
Love of nature; nobility; benevolence; magnificence
Light pink to purple

PLATE 13

Narcissus *(Narcissus poeticus)*
Stay as sweet as you are; formality; egotism
Snow-white petals with a yellow center rimmed in red

PLATE 14

Buttercup *(Ranunculus lingua)*
You are radiant with charm; riches
Bright yellow

PLATE 15

Yellow Rose *(Rosa maigold)*
Jealousy; let us forget; love waning
Yellow

PLATE 16

Trumpet Daffodil *(Narcissus spp.)*
Chivalry; deceitful; hope; unrequited love; regard
Generally yellow or white

PLATE 17

Tulip *(Tulipa spp.)*
Declaration of love; believe me; perfect lover; fame
Many colors, such as red, pink, yellow, and white, as well as
striped and speckled combinations of colors

PLATE 18

Hibiscus *(Hibiscus rosa-sinensis)*
Delicate beauty
Many colors, such as red, orange, blue, and white

PLATE 19

Pansy *(Viola spp.)*
Thoughtful recollection
Many colors, such as yellow, white, blue, and purple

PLATE 20

Zinnia *(Zinnia hybrid)*
Thoughts of absent friends; lasting affection; goodness; constancy
Many colors, such as coral, lavender, pale green, and apricot

PLATE 21

Jasmine *(Jasminum nudiflorum)*
Grace; elegance
Yellow

PLATE 22

Cornflower *(Centaurea cyanus)*
Delicacy; refinement
Blue-violet, blue, white, and pink

PLATE 23

Passionflower *(Passiflora caerulea)*
Faith; holy love; religious fervor
White, violet-blue, and blue

PLATE 24

Geranium *(Pelargonium x hortorum)*
Melancholy; folly; stupidity
Many colors and combinations, such as red, violet, and blue

PLATE 25

Forget me not *(Myosotis spp.)*
Memories; constancy; true love
Blue, white, and pink

PLATE 26

Morning Glory *(Ipomoea learii)*
Affection; departure
Violet-blue

PLATE 27

Red Rose (*Rosa* x '*Alec's Red*')
I love you; unity; romance; respect
Crimson

PLATE 28

Anemone (*Anemone spp.*)
Finding hope; anticipation
White, yellowish, rose, red, purple, violet

PLATE 29

Gardenia *(Jasminoides fortuniana)*
Secret love; refinement; joy
Creamy white

PLATE 30